ON GOOD AND BAD NEGOTIATING

ANON

Translation and commentary by

Jonathan Sims

First published 2012 by lulu.com

The right of Jonathan Sims to be identified as the author of this work has been asserted by him in accordance with the Copyright, Designs and Patents Act 1988.

All rights reserved. No part of this publication may be reproduced, stored in a retrieval system, or transmitted in any form or by any means, electronic, mechanical, photocopying, recording or otherwise, without the prior permission of the copyright owner.

ISBN 978-1-4710-3928-7

© Copyright 2012 Jonathan Sims (profitpie @ aol.com)

FOREWORD

In 2007 the tombs of two Japanese merchants were discovered in a small cemetery some two hundred kilometres from Tokyo. The dates of their deaths were not recorded but the style of their burial is in the traditional sixteenth century manner.

Out of customary respect to the deceased in Japan, I have changed their names to Ping and Pong.

Ping's tomb was ornate, filled with costly jewels, marble ornaments and portraits of happy loved ones to accompany Ping into the afterlife. Pong's tomb looked equally opulent but on closer inspection all the jewellery was found to be paste, ornaments of thin plaster and every picture was a self-portrait.

Of great interest was an urn buried between the two. It contained some hundred and thirty haikus on separate pages all concerning Ping and Pong. The author is anonymous but they are written by an educated hand. The title translates as "On Good and Bad Negotiating". It contains advice on successful and unsuccessful commercial negotiating which cover three main spheres: mental attitude, behaviour and technique.

The pages were piled in no apparent system. To give some semblance of order I have arranged them into a broad spectrum moving through Attitude of Mind to Behaviour and on to Technique. There are many grey areas and overlaps: for example Facing Fears demands a courageous attitude of mind, brave behaviour and a technique of asking uncomfortable questions. The distinction between behaviour and technique is most often nebulous.

Attitude of mind is a fundamental of negotiation. Without it, behaviour and technique can be little more than parrot talk. If a person has a mental attitude that negotiations always end at the market price, then his corresponding behaviour will be mild and conciliatory and technique that of asking for a 'fair', modest price.

However there can be a feedback effect: if a person tries a different technique such as asking for an immodest price and it proves to be successful, then the reward can influence future behaviour and consequently attitude of mind. This will be reinforced if repeatedly asking for immodest prices proves successful.

I believe that the haikus are of equal relevance some five hundred years later. Much of the advice is hard-nosed and will be anathema to the modern, Western proponents of soft, non-confrontational, cooperative, concessionary, win-win negotiation which regularly turns out lambs to the slaughter in the commercial world. Closer examination however reveals a balanced and Adult approach:

> Ping both hard and soft.
> Pong soft when hardness needed.
> Pong often doormat.

The haikus are of the standard five, seven and five syllable format. They are unusual in that there are none of the traditional allusions to nature or the seasons. However, references to emotions abound for good and bad. This is addressed in one particular haiku:

> Pong's emotions reign.
> Ping's emotions held by reins.
> Pong hot head, Ping cool.

Translation from Japanese into English is always fraught with difficulty. Pictograms and alphabets make impossible bedfellows, but I believe that cultural differences are overstated: we have a common humanity and negotiation skills are human skills before cultural practices.

As always, literal translations have to cede to comprehensible ones. I take all responsibility for the compromises. Likewise, the occasional anachronism has been used for greater clarity: it is unlikely that business-class travel existed five centuries ago. Cars and champagne certainly didn't. The reference to John F Kennedy has been used make clear the reference to Je-If-Qu'ai, famous historical Japanese shogun.

With all of the above in mind, I can only repeat the words of Sir Francis Bacon, statesman and philosopher, and possible contemporary of Ping and Pong:

"Read, not to contradict and dispute, nor to believe and take for granted, nor to find talk and discourse, but to weigh and consider."

I believe you will find it worthwhile.

Jonathan Sims
Trelowen
2011

CONTENTS

	Page
Attitude of mind versus Technique	8
Negotiators at work and home	9
Driven people	10
Objective versus psychological power	11
Slaves to expectations. Testing assumptions	12
Markets	13
Fixed prices	14
Compromise	15
Indifference	16
Active buyers and sellers	17
Needs and weaknesses	18
Maximising profit	19
Negotiating in opponent's world	20
Keeping heads private	21
The time to make a profit is now	22
The time to cut our losses is now	23
Parent-Adult-Child	24
Fairness	25
Relationships in business	26
Empty winning	27
Let them feel the winner	28
Lose the argument, win the money	29
Quiet confidence	30
Burdens	31
Judgementalism	32
Ego control	33
Sense of face	34
Dealing with rejection	35
Beware happiness	36
Happiness versus analysis	37
Vanity of turnover	38
Company money and private money	39
Fears	40
Facing fears	41
Civilised behaviour	42
Lying	43
Punctuality	44
Intransigence and compromise	45
Flexibility of approach	46
Control of emotions	47
Tough, not nasty	48
Anger control	49

Comfort zones	50
Talking versus listening	51
Talking versus silence	52
Silence	53
Different kinds of silence	54
Ego biscuits	55
Talking versus listening	56
Real listening	57
Dangerous talking	58
The words behind the words	59
Stay quiet while thinking	60
Small talk	61
First words	62
Holding back first words	63
Valuable and valueless words	64
Rambling	65
Avoiding negativity	66
Interrupting	67
Explaining, justifying	68
Knocking the product	69
Dealing with knocking the product, Defending the indefensible	70
Opinions	71
Withholding information	72
Avoiding answering questions (tactic one)	73
Avoiding answering questions (tactic two)	74
Avoiding answering questions (tactic three)	75
Avoiding answering questions (tactic four)	76
Pointing out mistakes	77
Ignorance and intelligence	78
Win by losing	79
Making mistakes	80
Their world is the real one	81
Leave them feeling winners	82
Anger	83
Stubbornness versus intransigence	84
Trust	85
Suspicion	86
Frustration	87
Politeness	88
Digging in	89
Painted into a corner	90
Building bridges	91
Concessions	92
Threats	93
Control of non-verbals	94
Control of time	95

Preparation: maps and improvisation	96
Thinking on feet	97
Displays of wealth	98
Paraphernalia	99
Focusing on the opponent	100
Territories	101
Direct questions	102
Why and When	103
State assumptions as facts	104
Be specific	105
Firm numbers	106
Debate, maths, logic	107
Doing the maths	108
Bottom lines	109
Rejection their offers	110
Picking up the small change	111
Not ignoring the pennies	112
Splitting the difference	113
Using unround numbers	114
Opening ridiculously	115
Trading concessions	116
Trading the unimportant for the important	117
Ever smaller moves	118
The final momentum	119
Giving ranges	120
Adapting image	121
Repeating their numbers	122
Repeating our numbers	123
Walking out	124
Walking back in	125
Team discipline	126
Team leaders	127
Identifying the decision maker	128

FINAL WORDS

Integrity	129
Men and women	130

Pong thinks all technique,
Ping has Attitude of Mind.
Pong foundationless.

Commentary: as with many human endeavours such as sport or art, attitude of mind is the foundation of and key to effective negotiating. Without it, then the behaviours and techniques of negotiating are empty: people go through the motions of "if he says... then I say..." without any wish to excel. If one has the skill to ride a bicycle, but chooses not to, then the skill is useless.

Outside work, Pong stops
But Ping negotiates all.
Ping's attitude right.

Commentary: negotiating skills are not like a suit that one puts on in the morning and takes off when returning from the office. They are an attitude of mind that one takes into all negotiations, company and private.

Pong is driven man
Doesn't know what drives, can't stop.
Ping not driven, drives.

Commentary: many people are driven, especially at the top of the business tree, by motivations such as fear of poverty or hunger for social respect. "Driven" is often regarded as a complimentary description. Sadly, driven people are usually unaware of what drives them, and are unable to step out of the game. People who are in charge of themselves have real self awareness and they drive. Effective negotiators are dispassionate and can stand outside the game.

For Pong, big force wins.
For Ping, smarter power wins.
Difference in head.

Commentary: psychological power in negotiation is far stronger than objective power. It exists in the negotiator's head and negotiators either believe they have it, or they surrender it to the opponent.

Ping tests assumptions.
Pong Slave to Expectations.
Ping learns so much more.

Ping tests assumptions.
Pong Slave to Expectations.
Ping uncovers truth.

Commentary: these are two very similar haikus. A Slave to Expectations expects, for example, not to get a reply to a difficult question, so doesn't ask it. Or expects that the negotiation will end at fifty-fifty or at "market price" and that becomes self-fulfilling. Whether we like it or not, we do make assumptions in negotiation; the important thing is to test them.

Pong respects markets.
Ping tests if markets apply:
Sometimes exceptions.

Commentary: never assume the market rules, it often does, but test whether it rules by asking questions. Also, realise that there are not such things as "markets", there are real people who run markets.

Pong pays fixed prices.
Ping challenges price labels.
Often gets discount.

Commentary: western children grow up believing in three things – Father Christmas, fairy tales and fixed prices. They tend to grow out of the first two but hold the last dear. It is not clear how prevalent haggling might have been in Japan, but in Europe the overwhelming majority of retail transactions are done at the label price, dictated by the seller. What holds us back? Fear of looking greedy? Fear of a rejection? Fear of becoming a little wealthier?

Pong compromises.
Ping makes others compromise.
Pong will sell the farm.

Commentary: this is another fundamental of effective negotiation, namely that it is not about compromise but getting the opponent to compromise. "What's mine is mine, what's yours is negotiable."

Pong says he wants deal.
Ping shrugs. "Deal would be Okay
But no deal good too."

Commentary: the Law of Indifference is one of the most effective laws of successful negotiation. It is the ability to bluff that one doesn't need the product or deal, even if one is desperate for it. It does not have to be rude. In fact, polite indifference is a useful default setting.

Pong says he wants deal.
Ping says good, then sell to me.
Pong active seller.

Pong says he wants deal.
Ping says good, then buy from me.
Pong active buyer.

Commentary: in any negotiation at any point one party is actively doing the buying or the selling. If you're the buyer, make them sell to you. If you're the seller, make them buy from you. And avoid being the first to put the figure on the table.

Pong knows his weakness.
Ping knows Pong's needs and weakness.
Ping less weak than Pong.

Commentary: an interesting, unconventional view of negotiating. Normally it is regarded as an exercise of power, a struggle of strengths. The author seems to be implying that both sides knows their needs and weakness, but the more successful negotiators put theirs to one side, and play on the needs and weakness of the other side.

Pong eats minimum.
But Pong eyes up maximum.
Minimum thin soup.

Commentary: a slightly obscure haiku. It could be a premonition of the capitalist imperative that capitalism is not about simply making a profit, but of maximising profit, and that all employees working in a capitalist company have a duty to maximise for their employer.

Pong sees world his way.
Ping sees world the other's way.
Pong's world so blinkered.

Pong thinks his world real.
Ping perceives many real worlds
But Pong's good for now.

Pong lives in own head.
Ping lives inside Pong's own head.
Ping understands Pong.

Commentary: these three haikus deal with a similar theme. A successful negotiation takes place in the other person's head no matter how irrational, lazy, egotistical or stupid that head might be. A common error of negotiators is to assume that their opponents see the circumstances the same way; they don't and we must understand their world. There is no consensus reality. There are billions of realities imposed upon the world to allow people to cope with life.

Ping's head so private.
Pong's head big public highway
Wide open to all.

Commentary: getting inside the opponent's head is a key to effective negotiating. One of the most effective ways is to ask questions. As we will, see one of the skills of the successful negotiator is to avoid answering questions, thus keeping their needs and weaknesses to themselves. Equally, a successful negotiator will realise that if he gets emotional or angry, he has allowed the opponent to get inside his head. Remember: "No one is allowed in my head without my permission".

Pong profits "one day".
Ping makes profit here and now.
Pong hungry today.

Commentary: the time to make a profit is now. So often, for example, special low prices are offered in the hope of making profits in the future that never arrive. "I was thinking of the long term" is one of the most common post-rationalisations for poor negotiating.

Ping cuts losses now.
Pong calls losses "investments".
Pong eats small dinner.

Commentary: reflecting the previous haiku, the time to cut your losses is now. Something inveterate losing gamblers forget. However, so often in business, losses are rationalised as investments in the future, but continue to erode profits.

Ping learning Adult.
Pong pompous Parent, mean Child.
Adults are winners.

Commentary: Transactional Analysis five hundred years before its time! The Parent is judgemental, all-knowing, blinkered, often pompous. The Child can be spiteful and destructive. The effective negotiator is in the Adult state: learning, balancing, experimenting with new things. The Adult, however, might use Parent or Child behaviour when appropriate.

> Pong calls for fairness.
> Ping knows fair's for kids and crooks.
> Fair means 'fair for me'.

Commentary: the skilled negotiator's ears will prick up on hearing the word 'fair'. It's a word for conmen and children. "I'm sure you will agree this is a fair offer" means that it's advantageous for the speaker. "Come on, you're not being fair here" is the appeal of a loser for altruism. It's a powerful word which reaches us from school playgrounds, but on analysis is a very flexible, if not empty, word which means whatever the user wants. A hoorah word. What is a fair rent? The market price? The government-dictated price? What the renter can pay and live comfortably? What the landlord needs to make a reasonable return on the investment? Take your pick.

Pong likes to be liked
But Ping sees relationships
As means to profit.

Commentary: a hard-hearted but realistic view of negotiating. Many people (salespeople, relationship bank managers) so often see the nurturing a good relationship as the end in itself. It certainly feels good. But it has to have a final aim of making profit, maximising profit in fact.

Pong loves to feel win.
Ping thinks winning for children.
Pong childish winner.

Pong left with baubles
Feeds ego, child, pomposity.
Ping feels full wallet.

Commentary: it is the Child in us that loves to feel that we've won in negotiation but so often these wins are the baubles and symbols of victory such as ego-feeding. The Adult will dispassionately aim to gain the maximum of financial and non-financial advantage from the negotiating table. Competitive people usually make the best salesmen and the worst negotiators: they can be easily manipulated to take their eyes off the main prize on the table and try to win those symbols of victory.

Pong celebrates win.
Ping congratulates Pong's win.
Who's the real winner?

Commentary: at the end of a negotiation it is often necessary to find a formula of words to congratulate the opponent on a hard-earned victory. If you think you've gained everything, never crow about it (some negotiators do) because people can be remarkably destructive and spiteful if they think they've been driven to do a bad deal.

Pong wins arguments.
Ping loses all empty points.
Eyes money firmly.

Commentary: an effective negotiator will be perfectly happy to lose all the arguments, debates, points of detail. These are all "wins" for poor negotiators. The successful negotiator will simply aim to take all the money (and non-financials) from the table.

Pong's confidence loud.
Ping still, collected, silent.
True confidence calm.

Commentary: effective negotiators usually have a quiet self-assurance. Insecure negotiators usually make the most noise.

Pong carries burdens.
Ping leaves burdens on roadside.
Burdens crush poor Pong.

Commentary: burdens include giving answers, providing explanations and justifications, offering apologies, doing the maths. Effective negotiators do not carry these burdens, or at least choose to carry them only occasionally and for a short time.

Pong is judgemental.
Ping can suspend all judgement:
Neither right nor wrong.

Commentary: the appropriate attitude is "I do what I do, He does what He does". The opponent is neither right nor wrong, clever nor stupid. He does what He does and we learn from it.

Pong upholds his ego.
Ping leaves ego at the door.
Pong's ego costs him.

Ping's pride waits outside.
Pong's ego sits on shoulders.
Pong's ego costs loads.

Commentary: Ego is a compensation mechanism for deep feelings of inferiority. So much of political and trade union is primarily about upholding and feeding the egos of the actors involved. Ego leads people to feel great about poor results, or walk away from perfectly good deals.

Pong keeps sense of face.
Ping feeds Pong's face, forgets own.
Pong pays dear for face.

Commentary: the notion of a sense of face is well-known in oriental negotiations. It can be equally important in Western negotiations and is a close cousin to ego. An effective negotiator will treat the opponent's face with kid gloves, doing all possible to avoid creating defensiveness, while regarding his own sense of face as irrelevant.

Pong hates rejection.
Ping takes rejection on chin.
Pong nice guy but poor.

Commentary: an ability to cope with the fear of rejection is the defining skill of the successful salesman. An effective negotiator will often use subtle alternations of acceptance and rejection to handle the opponent.

When Pong glad, he's glad.
When Ping glad, feels unhappy
Because more to take.

Commentary: "When you're feeling happy, feel unhappy, because you've probably left money on the table". When feeling happy, most negotiators start winding down. Effective negotiators keep pushing for more, staying outside their comfort zones.

Pong goes home happy.
Ping just ponders what happened.
Pong happy but poor.

Commentary: most negotiators write off the last deal as a success or failure. Skilled negotiators will analyse what happened and what improvements they can make to their performance next time, particularly with the same opponent.

Pong loves turnover.
Ping loves profit and payment.
Pong collects Fool's Gold.

Commentary: a forerunner of the modern maxim "Turnover is Vanity, Profit is Sanity, Cash is Reality".

Ping saves expenses.
Pong wastes company money.
Ping's company rich.

Ping values money.
Pong loves his expense account.
Ping retires wealthy.

Commentary: many business people think that there are two types of money – their own money and company money. We have a duty to be as careful with company money as we are with our own, but so much of management is a conspiracy of theft against the shareholders: people using company money to buy comforts and perks (business class travel, top of the range cars, fine dining, five star hotels) which they do not do with their own money. One cannot be an effective negotiator with such an attitude of mind. Moreover, a person reliant on the expense account to enjoy luxury is unlikely to become genuinely rich.

Ping feels fear but acts.
Pong freezes and fears control.
Fears lead Pong to lose.

Ping calls fears liars.
Pong pretends they don't exist
But lead him by nose.

Commentary: people rarely think about fear being a factor in negotiation, but if they have enough self-awareness they could probably identify some ten or twenty fears they walk in with. The fear of: blowing the deal; blowing the whole business; rejection; failure; losing the relationship; reprimand from the boss; ridicule of colleagues; appearing greedy; appearing weak; appearing overbearing; appearing stupid; being unprepared. And on and on. The point is that these fears are only real because we make them real. They only exist in our head and we can equally well make them unreal. The effective negotiator will realise that the opponent has ten or twenty fears of his own, often identical, and will play on those fears in negotiation.

Ping faces dark fears.
Pong carries fears on shoulders.
Ping's fears disappear.

Pong fears bad answers.
Ping faces fears, asks questions.
Pong can never learn.

Commentary: the way to deal with fears is not to suppress or ignore them, but to face them. Face your fears. If there's a question you don't want ask, ask it. If there's a topic you fear bringing up, bring it up. Eight times out of ten the reality will be a fraction of what you feared.

Pong so civilised.
Ping ignores rules if needed.
Pong polite but skint.

Commentary: the values of civilisation include selflessness, collaboration, rationality, humility, truthfulness. Whether we like it or not, the tools of negotiation can be diametrically opposed. They include selfishness, independence, emotion, arrogance, deceitfulness. This is neither right nor wrong; it just is. Like the weather. The inability to recognise this is a huge inhibition to negotiators.

Ping knows people lie.
Pong "conceals" "exaggerates"
But, in truth, he lies.

Commentary: despite the protestations of the proponents of "principled negotiation", in reality negotiation is a process of subtle and not-so-subtle lying between two parties. To save feelings, we call it bending the truth, being economical with the truth, concealing inconvenient facts, telling white lies, putting spin on things. But it is, in fact, lying. The inability to recognise this is an important inhibiting factor for negotiators.

Pong unpunctual.
Ping might be late if chooses
But mainly on time.

Commentary: punctuality is not so much a question of simple achievability but rather an attitude of mind. People are usually late because they are not in charge of themselves. An effective negotiator might choose to be late either to demonstrate indifference to the deal or even to the opponent, but otherwise will choose to be on time.

Ping stands on firm ground.
Pong hurries to the middle
Then further to Ping.

Commentary: intransigence is a fundamental attribute in effective negotiation. The message is: I stand here, if you want a deal then you have to walk to me. Those who believe that negotiation is compromise and that they have an obligation to walk to the middle ground, and then even further, are losers.

Ping both hard and soft.
Pong soft when hardness needed.
Pong often doormat.

Commentary: successful negotiation demands flexibility of approach – combining hard with soft skills. Those who have only been taught the soft skills are so often like lambs to the slaughter.

Pong's emotions reign.
Ping's emotions held by reins.
Pong hot head, Ping cool.

Commentary: contrary to what many may think, negotiation can be a quagmire of competing emotions – fear, anger, happiness, competitiveness. Those aware of this can more easily control the destructive emotions which militate against success. Effective negotiators might feign strong emotions when appropriate but will never be overtaken by them.

Pong's rude and nasty.
Ping always tough and firm but
Not rude or nasty.

Commentary: strong negotiators are often tough and firm, but never nasty or rude. Many of them in fact seem like the very milk of human kindness.

Pong does get so mad.
JFK said get even.
Ping merely gets rich.

Commentary: John F Kennedy's dictum "don't get mad, get even" was inappropriate to effective negotiators, even to those from fabulously wealthy, arrogant families. They simply leave egos at the door and get on with maximising advantage. If the opponent feels good by getting even, so be it.

Pong in comfort zone.
Ping sits in stress, discomfort.
Pong comfy but poor.

Commentary: skilled negotiation is stressful. We are aiming to maximise advantage rather than settle for the comfortable fifty percent. We are asking some very blunt questions. We might be making 'unreasonable' demands. We are working against our opponents manipulating us. We need to be prepared to work outside our comfort zones. "We are paid to feel uncomfortable".

Pong has one big mouth.
Ping little mouth, two big ears.
Ears outnumber mouths.

Commentary: the modern saying is "we have two ears and one mouth, and should use them in that proportion". This probably overestimates the use we should make of our mouths.

When weak Pong talks more.
Ping silent or asks questions.
Ping's power returns.

Commentary: poor negotiators talk more the less secure they feel and this is when all the dangerous words and comments come out. When effective negotiators feel on the back foot, the best policy is to fall silent or ask a question, and they feel the power return.

Ping's silences are steel.
Pong's words like soggy cabbage.
Silence is a knife.

Commentary: silence can be the strongest form of attack. If feeling weak, fall silent. Most people cannot bear the burden of silence and fill it with the sound of their voices. It can be most effective on the telephone.

Pong's silence all ego.
Ping's silence active, working.
Pong's silence wasted.

Commentary: there are two main types of silence – an egotistical "damned if I'm going to talk" silence, and an active, non-egotistical silence. If your opponent has fallen for the first, choose to help him off his high horse and ask a question.

Ping eats info up.
Pong devours ego biscuits.
Pong's fat, poor ego!

Ping's ego biscuits
Are cooked specially for Pong.
Pong eats them all up.

Commentary: 'ego biscuits' are the nearest translated approximation I can make to the original concept of 'face cakes'. Those acquainted with training dogs, dolphins or performing seals might be acquainted with the idea. They are the titbits used to reward behaviour. Ego biscuits in negotiations are things such as letting the opponent have the first word, last word, smart arse remark, finding spelling mistakes, dictating the time and place of the negotiation, just to impose their egos. The effective negotiator will let them have all this, but takes all the money on the table.

Ping asks Pong to talk.
Pong thinks talking shows power.
Ping glad to listen.

Commentary: who talks first in a negotiation is an important sub-negotiation. In general, invite the opponent to start talking first. It reveals preoccupations and gives information. Information really is power. If you're negotiating with someone who believes talking is dominating – great !

Ping listens with care.
Pong hears what he wants to hear.
Only Ping's learning.

Commentary: in the stress of a negotiation we tend to develop tunnel hearing similar to tunnel vision. We tend to hear what we want to hear, or when feeling defensive or belligerent, we hear what we don't want to hear or can take offence at.

Pong talks when nervous.
Ping falls silent when unsure.
Pong gives game away.

When stumped, Ping silent.
When clueless, Pong chatters on.
Ping gives away less.

While Ping listens more
Pong thinks talk means dominate.
Ping learns so much more.

Pong's words say nothing.
Ping's loud silence speak volumes.
Power simply quiet.

Commentary: in fact, silence dominates, not talking. We never talk so much as when we are not sure what to say. There is nearly always an inverse relationship between talking and power.

Pong rarely hears words.
Ping hears words behind the words.
Pong lives in deaf world.

Commentary: Listening, real active listening is a rare skill and rarer still amongst egocentric negotiators. We need to be listening not only for the words themselves, but also for the subtexts and hidden agendas: the words behind the words.

Ping shuts mouth to think.
Pong talks while deciding words.
Pong an open book.

Commentary: there is little more dangerous in negotiating than talking while making one's mind up what to say. That's when all the little truths slip out. When you've got nothing to say, say nothing. If you have to wait five minutes to construct a sentence, wait five minutes.

Ping's small talk has aim.
Pong's like piss in howling gale.
Pong's trousers get wet.

Commentary: initial small talk is usually pointless. Its purpose is to make the speaker feel comfortable, not the listener. "How are you doing?" is a wet question. "How did you get here today?" or "Where have you come from?" might elicit more useful information.

Ping chooses first words.
Pong opens mouth randomly.
First words can destroy.

Commentary: the first words of a negotiation set the scene and can determine the final outcome. An inappropriate comment or joke can sink a negotiation before it has even properly started.

Pong walks in and talks.
Ping walks in and waits for talk:
Perhaps concessions?

Commentary: this is one of the less clear haikus. I think it concerns the inclination of people who, having called a time-out, return to the negotiating table and start talking as if they need to justify their time away. In fact it is much more useful to return and wait for the other party to talk – they might have been deciding on a concessionary move.

Ping's words like gold dust.
Pong's words like goat's turds on fan:
Most return on face.

Commentary: most negotiators are very lax with their words. They think of the general sense of what they want to say and grab words like a handful of mud, then throw it at the subject in the hope that the general meaning sticks. The effective negotiator knows that the less you say, the greater the impact.

Pong talks round houses,
Up hill, through trees, down river.
Ping short, sharp, shut up.

Commentary: poor negotiators love the sound of their voices, their eloquence and flowery language. It is usually caused however by the stress of the situation and inability to ask a straight question. "What's your price?" becomes "If you don't mind me asking, could you could give me a ballpark indication of what sort of price you might be considering, if it's not a rude question."

Ping sparing with No's.
Pong loves negatives.
Positive spin wins.

Commentary: even in collaborative contexts, many people show a natural inclination towards negativity in negotiation. They are happier to tell what's unacceptable, rather than what's acceptable, what they can't do rather than what they can do. Effective negotiators save No's for very special occasions, come back with positivity in the face of the opponent's habitual negativity, put a positive spin on all they say. They don't say "we're still miles apart" but rather "I think we can get closer together".

Pong will interrupt.
Ping waits 'til they've stopped talking.
Worth interrupting?

Commentary: never interrupt your opponents. They might give you important information. Don't even interrupt to correct a factual mistake: wait till they've finished speaking, then judge whether it's worth putting them right. It usually isn't.

Pong argues, explains,
Qualifies and justifies.
Ping gives nought away.

Pong explains demands.
Ping just says "it's what I want".
Pong blown from water.

Commentary: never explain, justify or qualify. The opponent is not listening for reasons to be persuaded but to find flaws in your words, arguments, maths and logic that can be used against you. The less you say, the less you give away.

Even if product's perfect.
Ping finds reason to knock it.
But Pong salivates.

Commentary: it is perfectly appropriate for buyers to "knock" the product even if it meets all their requirements. Find reasons to criticise. Work out what weakness the seller might fear in his product.

Pong defends weakness.
Ping grants what's indefensible.
Pong's weaknesses grow.

If Pong knocks product
Ping smiles and agrees with him.
End of argument.

Commentary: when your product, service or position is being 'knocked', it is only natural to defend it. Or salespeople say turn the disadvantage into an advantage. The most effective way of dealing with it is to agree and add the rider 'that's all taken into account in the price' or 'that's why the price is so reasonable'. Don't defend the indefensible.

Ping asks poor Pong's views.
Pong so opinionated.
Opinions dear.

Commentary: five hundred years on, the age of opinionation is even more prevalent. Opinions betray what is more important to the individual than what's on the table. It might be simple ego-satisfaction. Effective negotiators invite the opponent to express opinions whilst keeping theirs strictly to themselves. They are thinking: "What's more important to that person than the money?"

For information
Pong big Information Desk.
Ping dry oasis.

Commentary: effective negotiators keep their positions to themselves and reveal the bare minimum about their needs. Poor negotiators reveal their hands very quickly.

Pong answers questions.
Ping talks about the weather.
Pong gives all away.

If Pong asks question
Ping changes subject around.
Pong natters again.

Commentary: avoid answering questions. Answering questions is a social burden that we have carried since childhood. We believe it part of our function in life to give answers and supply other people with information. Its danger in negotiation should be self-evident. Even answering with a lie is dangerous because, if the opponent is focusing on you, a lie will tell as much as the truth.
Tactic One: change the subject.

If Pong ask question
Ping replies Why do you ask?
Pong chatters again.

Commentary: avoid answering questions.
Tactic Two: bounce back a question and return the burden on their shoulders.

If Pong asks question
Ping postpones an answer for
Ever and ever.

Commentary: avoid answering questions.
Tactic Three: say you'll come back to it later. Perhaps compliment them on the pertinence of the question. Then forget it. A politician's favourite.

If Pong asks question
Ping sometimes answers question.
But different one.

Commentary: avoid answering questions.
Tactic Four: answer a different question, one that suits you. Another politician's favourite, much used by Margaret Thatcher.

Pong points out mistake.
Ping hears mistake, stays silent.
Pong smartarse none loves.

Commentary: it's ego (a mechanism to compensate for fundamental insecurity) that drives people to point out mathematical and spelling mistakes committed by the opponent. Worse still, grammatical mistakes. They are unimportant but make egotists feel important. They do it often to belittle or anger the other side which is rarely appropriate. Effective negotiators listen for mistakes to see if there is any advantage in them, but stay silent. If their mistakes are pointed out to them, they listen politely but stay concentrated on gaining what's available on the table. They are happy to feed the opponent with ego biscuits.

Ping says "I don't know".
Pong shows off intelligence.
Pong smartarse but poor.

Commentary: a self-assured negotiator is perfectly prepared to admit ignorance, rather than dangerously feigning knowledge. Knowing things, being intelligent is another burden that the effective negotiator is happy to drop. "I don't know" can be our three best friends in sticky situations.

Pong adores winning.
Ping sometimes wins by losing.
Lose battle, win war.

Commentary: effective negotiators are perfectly happy to grant all the petty ego victories to the opponent. They're there to take all the money off the table.

> If Ping makes mistake
> Ping just withdraws from mistake.
> Pong tied to mistakes.

Commentary: even the best negotiators make mistakes. They might, for example, make a larger concession than they had intended. The poor negotiator feels tied to that mistake for fear of appearing stupid or greedy. These fears are immaterial to effective negotiators who simply admit to the mistake. If necessary, they attach an impossible condition to their offer which they know the other cannot comply with: "that million dollars has to be paid in thirty minutes in used, untraceable twenty dollar bills ... you can't do that? Then my previous two million dollars has to stand."

Pong thinks the world flat.
To get deal, Ping agrees with him.
Pong glad to be right.

Commentary: a negotiation takes place in the opponent's head, in the opponent's world. What we take to be our knowledge, which is often equally an assembly of delusion, is immaterial to the negotiation. See the world the way they see it.

Pong celebrates win.
Ping congratulates Pong's win.
Who's the real winner?

Commentary: leave the opponent delighted to have won all the symbols of victory. This is often helped by a carefully chosen formula of words at the end. Such as "We're not happy with it but we think we can live with it. We look forward to working with you".

Pong quick to anger.
Pong pretends to be angry.
Real anger costs dear.

Ping can act angry.
Pong genuinely angry.
Pong angry, hungry.

Commentary: as with fear, anger is an emotion that is rarely associated with negotiation, but it is often there. It is often rationalised and diminished as frustration or irritation. Often it is directed at oneself. It is destructive and reduces the skills of the negotiator. The skilled negotiator might feign anger when appropriate, but if they are genuinely angry, they have let the opponent inside their heads. Then they remember that "Nobody is allowed inside my head without my permission."

Pong is so stubborn.
Ping can show intransigence.
That's intelligent.

Commentary: Intransigence is a fundamental behaviour of negotiation. It should not however be confused with stubbornness which is merely stupid and egotistic.

Pong demands their trust.
Ping gets trust by giving trust.
Trust can't be assumed.

Commentary: trust is the lifeblood of collaborative negotiation. But it can't be expected or demanded. It can only be gained by showing trust. Tokens of trust at first, building up to a framework of trust within which both parties can work. It is fragile and can be easily destroyed.

Pong so suspicious
But Ping only monitors.
Suspicion erodes.

Commentary: if trust is the lifeblood of collaborative negotiation, then suspicion is the cancer of it. A sceptical rather than cynical stance is called for. People can be remarkably destructive when suspicious. But again we cannot expect or demand that suspicion be dropped by the opponent. We overcome it by truth and tokens of trust.

Pong oft frustrated.
Ping has infinite patience.
"Recalculating".

Commentary: the ability to cope with frustration, to have that almost infinite patience to put a deal together, is the hallmark of the effective negotiator. In fact, the negotiator will have done so much thorough preparation that he will have the ability to recalculate routes with the patience of the car satellite navigation device.

Pong always polite.
Ping polite to get the deal.
Polite needs a point.

Commentary: one of the fundamental attitudes of mind is that I Owe Nobody Anything. We do not owe the opponent an explanation, justification, apology or even the end of our sentence. We might extend politeness to them to achieve the deal, but it is a means to an end. We do not a priori owe them politeness.

In holes, Pong digs in.
In holes, Ping stops digging.
Holes too expensive.

Commentary: if something's not working, stop and try something else. However, so often it seems human nature to continue the same behaviour as if afraid to waste the unsuccessful investment.

In painted corner
Pong freezes against the wall.
Ping walks through the paint.

Commentary: certain phrases in negotiation should be avoided such as "is that your final offer?" or "take it or leave it." If their egos are involved, then their answers are predictable. However, the effective negotiator who has ego under control is perfectly happy to walk through the paint and continue negotiating.

Pong builds high strong walls.
Ping builds bridges for Pong's ease.
Bridges beat big walls.

Commentary: whilst intransigence is a quality of the effective negotiator, it is different from the stubbornness which favours negativity and the word "No". Particularly in the middle game of negotiation, skilled negotiators will be creating bridges for the opponent to cross towards them.

Ping gives just enough.
Pong concedes shedloads too quick.
Pong's sheds soon empty.

Commentary: knowing how little to concede and how often is a fundamental skill of negotiation. Big, generous moves can merely make the opponent greedy for more. We need to ask ourselves "what is the minimum I need to give to show good faith and keep the momentum going?"

Pong threatens with fist.
Ping threatens with suggestions.
Smiles can be threats too.

Commentary: like it or not, so much of negotiation is about promises and threats. A promise is an offer which appeals to the opponent's self-interest. A threat need not be a fist in the opponent's face, but sometimes merely an indication that it would be more pleasant to do what is suggested than not to do it.

Ping controls body.
Pong throws hands and feet around.
Pong easy to read.

Commentary: the ability to read non-verbal signals on a conscious level and also to 'write' them, is huge advantage to the negotiator. However, most people are unaware of the signals they are emitting and only read their opponent's body language on an unconscious level.

Ping controls the time.
Ping pisses the time away.
But time is money.

Commentary: control of time is a fundamental skill of negotiation, as hostage negotiators know. Certainly, there is a final momentum in those last seconds when money is given away unnecessarily. Be careful however than any time pressures you might try to exercise on the opponent do not work against you as well.

Pong prepares a route.
Ping considers the what-ifs.
Pong lands in dark ditch.

Ping always prepares.
Pong makes it up on the hoof.
Ping is much stronger.

Commentary: preparation is 90% of negotiation and of that 90%, 90% should be done inside the opponent's head. Preparation is about making maps, not routes, when as many what-ifs are covered as possible to make up a thorough picture. The aim is "No Surprises".

Pong thinks fast on feet.
Ping postpones tricky answers.
Pong's feet trip him up.

Commentary: effective negotiators know that unprepared off-pat answers are often dangerous, and are happy to take time out to consider.

Pong comes in flash car.
Ping parks car round the corner.
Pong no mystery.

Pong wears such smart clothes.
Ping wears less smart clothes than Pong.
Pong can win that one.

Commentary: displays of wealth often backfire in negotiation. It can be very difficult for some companies to plead poverty whilst displaying the trappings of opulence.

Pong carries briefcase.
Ping takes in smallest notepad.
Ping professional.

Commentary: what paraphernalia we take in with us should be carefully considered. Arms full of briefcases and files can actually make us appear quite junior. A small notepad is often enough and makes us look powerful and prepared.

Pong stares at his notes.
Ping observes words and gestures.
Pong sees so little.

Commentary: we learn so much more by focusing on the opponent rather than staring at our own notes.

Pong says "come to me".
Ping goes to him and learns lots.
Pong learns nought at home.

Commentary: where the negotiation takes place is an important sub-negotiation. Conventional advice is to have the meeting on one's own territory, but this can lead to several disadvantages: a complacent comfort factor; interruptions; lack of preparation and analysis; the presence of unhelpful people or information. We learn so much more by going to see the opponent and it might be an ego biscuit we can throw to them.

Ping asks straight questions.
Pong asks whether he can ask.
Ping gets more answers.

Commentary: there is a big difference between "what's your price?" and "do you mind if I ask what your price is?" The latter introduces a note of embarrassment, subservience and gives the opponent more time to think.

Ping asks Why? and When?
Pong tells why, when and how urgent.
Ping holds all aces.

Commentary: the Why and the When are the two most important questions in negotiation. The Why makes people most defensive and might have to be patiently wheedled out. People are more ready to reveal time limits which in turn reveal urgency. Skilled negotiators will often use the time limits sound like a disadvantage which will cost the opponent money. Skilled negotiators will keep their Why and When close to their chests. They appear indifferent and to have all the time in the world.

To find out secrets
Ping states assumptions as facts.
Pong asks lame questions.

Commentary: questions such as "are you in a hurry to sell your house?' invite a simple denial. Go fishing. State the assumption as a fact: "I hear from the real estate agent that you're keen to move soon, I think I can help...." Do they challenge the assumption or let it through? Half the time your statements will miss the mark, but half the time you'll learn something important.

Pong's talk all so vague.
Ping talks in strong specifics.
They mean so much more.

Commentary: short, sharp and shut up. Short, sharp and sweet if appropriate. Use direct questions. Give specific numbers. Numbers speak louder than words. Don't mistake politeness with the number of words. Flabby talk is for the nervous and insecure.

Ping gives strong prices.
Pong makes offers, proposals,
And weak suggestions.

Commentary: use hard words for your numbers – 'price', 'cost', 'figure'. Refer to the opponent's numbers as offers, proposals or suggestions. These are weak words which you should avoid when referring to your numbers.

Pong's great debater.
Pong wins all the great debates.
Ping wins the money.

Pong uses maths, logic.
Ping tells What's in it for them.
Maths and logic don't win.

Commentary: sometimes three quarters of the negotiating time is spent debating. People seem to think that the power of their argument, the merits of their case will be enough to convince the opponent. They won't. People are listening for mistakes in the opponents' maths and logic to use against them. People are moved by threats to or fulfilment of their self interest. That ugly old question "What's in it for me?" so disdained by win-win proponents.

Ping does maths in head.
Pong pulls out his abacus
Does maths for them all.

Commentary: doing the maths in the negotiation is one of those burdens the effective negotiator declines to carry. Don't do their maths for them. Do the maths in your head or outside the room, but don't become the numbers-wallah. Let them do the maths and they might make a mistake in your favour. If it's to your disadvantage, point it out.

Ping sets firm limit.
Pong has so soft bottom line.
Pong a pushover.

Commentary: setting a firm bottom line, or top line, or crunch point, or walk-away point, or exit point, or must-have, or minimum selling price or maximum buying price is a fundamental task of the effective negotiator. It needs to arrived at dispassionately and egolessly. No bottom line is even more dangerous than a soft bottom line. But having set it, we need to take our eyes off it and aim for the opponent's bottom line because our job is to maximise advantage, not just get the deal.

Ping holds back the price.
Pong offers opener first.
Ping ridicules it.

Pong puts first offer.
Ping laughs oh so politely.
Then Pong doubts himself.

Commentary: we have an undoubted advantage getting the opponent to put his offer on the table first. And, whatever it is, dismiss it in the appropriate terms; "How much!" "You've got to be joking!" There's always more to come. A salesman's first price is always a lie.

Ping picks up small change.
Ping gives final concessions.
Ping's pockets well filled.

Commentary: picking up the small change, that final little concession, that extra one percent, can mean all the difference in business between making margin or not. The small change is that little bit they'll give to avoid losing the deal.

Pong talks millions.
Ping talks millions and pence.
Picks up big and small.

Commentary: the way people refer to money is a big indication of their sense of slack in money. To refer to thousands as 'k's' or 'grands' shows contempt for a lot of money and demonstrates little concern for the hundreds. A hundred dollars is a hundred dollars whether it's on a dinner for two or a hundred million dollar deal – it's still worth going for.

Ping never agrees
To splitting the difference.
Pong does. And loses.

Commentary: "Shall we split the difference?" is a tactic often used in the final moments of a negotiation. What it really means is "I've got what I want and I'm going to take you for more". You might have to go a short distance or throw an ego biscuit to save their feelings, but never move 50%. On the other hand, if you think you might gain that little bit more, try saying it.

Pong rounds up and down.
Ping's numbers all come out odd.
Sound more considered.

Commentary: use odd numbers with little bits at the end such as 'five hundred and sixty three dollars, thirty-six cents". Such a price might be completely arbitrary but carries authority.

Pong opens modest.
Ping starts ridiculously.
Ping has room to move.

Pong opens fairly.
Ping opens ridiculous.
They end in middle.

Commentary: opening "ridiculously" (beyond the opponent's limit) is a fundamental skill of the effective negotiator. It gives room to manoeuvre, often leads to self-doubt in the opponent, and gives the opportunity to maximise advantage. Many negotiations end somewhere in the middle of the opening positions, therefore the person who opens more extreme tends to end up with more of what's available on the table.

Pong gives concessions.
Ping says "If you...then we will..."
Ping trades concessions.

Commentary: this trade is a basic human behaviour but is so often ignored in negotiation where people tend to give straight concessions. The trade pulls something back for everything it gives. It makes each concession conditional on accepting the less sweet pill. You also show that you never give anything for nothing.

Pong trades importants
Against Ping's unimportants.
Clever trade for Ping

Commentary: the real art of the trade is to identify which items are unimportant or of lesser importance to you and to exchange them for those things that are important to you that your opponent considers unimportant. Usually people are poor at this: they fail to appreciate the different world of the other side, thus misjudging their priorities and then giving away things that night be unimportant for them but could be vital for the other. Thus the cash-rich negotiator might concede immediate payment when he could have traded it for, say, an extension of guarantee.

Pong concedes by strides.
Ping strides, then steps, then shuffles.
Pong cedes much further.

Commentary: effective negotiators' concessions get smaller and smaller, rather than regular, or worse still, bigger and bigger. They give the impression that they are making generous strides towards the opponent, but in fact they are getting meaner and meaner.

Ping slows down at end.
Pong rushes final moments.
Ping picks up margin.

At end Pong bites hand.
Ping stops, waits and takes teeth out.
Says No to get more.

Commentary: there is a final momentum in many negotiations where the poor negotiator gets excited for the deal and gives unnecessary concessions. Effective negotiators will ignore the time pressure and use the momentum to pick up the small change.

Pong gives a weak range.
Ping says a single figure.
Ping likes to hear range.

Commentary: don't give ranges such as "we're looking for four to five thousand." State a single figure. If you hear a range, pick the number you like.

Pong plays same old Pong.
Ping adapts image to suit.
Same Pong a poor man.

Commentary: very few people give conscious thought to what image would be most advantageous in this negotiation with this person. We have a range of images we might adopt between aggression and mild cooperation. Equally, we need to think about what atmosphere is most appropriate. However we tend to play the same old us and leave the atmosphere to chance.

Pong repeats Ping's price.
Pong's price like soap in Ping's mouth.
Will never say it.

Commentary: don't repeat the opponent's figure. It gives it a level of credibility even if we are ridiculing it. Call it "that" or "that price".

Pong says Ping's figure.
Now Ping knows he will pay it.
Repeat means accept.

Commentary: generally, people seldom mention unacceptable figures. If they mention a figure, the chances are they would settle for it. Try it out.

Pong never walks out.
Ping has a walk-away price.
Pong weak prisoner.

Commentary: unless we have a real walk-away limit, we can't negotiate. Also, walking out can be a strong move in negotiation, but few do it. They fear appearing rude. They fear losing the relationship. They fear not being called back. They fear looking weak if they return. All these fears are real but self-created.

After walking out
Pong feels weak if returning.
Ping just walks back in.

Commentary: if we've walked out but still want to do the deal, don't let our egos keep us out. Equally, if the opponent has walked out but we still want to do the deal, don't let our egos stop us getting them back. We're employed to make business deals, not ego deals. We're only weak if we let ourselves feel weak.

Pong's team all chatter.
Ping's team shows strong self-control.
Pong's team all at sea.

Commentary: one of the few references to team negotiations in the manuscript. It is possible that neither Ping nor Pong had much opportunity to use teams but their advantage for us can be overwhelming. A single negotiator has to do all the thinking, planning, talking, observing and numbers. A lot for one person to do. A rehearsed, disciplined, role-aware team increases its power by the number of people on the team. An unprepared, undisciplined team where everyone feels entitled to butt in when they please is reduced to the strength of its weakest link. Part of a disciplined team's job is to encourage all the opponents to talk – usually like shooting fish in a barrel.

Ping quiet leader.
Pong leads, talks and overrides.
Pong's team is so weak.

Commentary: it is a common team failing to let the leader also be the spokesperson, usually for reasons of ego. Often in business the boss is the least acquainted with the situation. The leader should be too busy with planning to talk. The spokesperson is too busy delivering to plan. And why keep dogs and bark yourself?

Ping asks who is boss?
Pong assumes boss wears best suit.
Pong so often wrong.

Commentary: a first priority in team negotiation is to learn the roles of all the other side and to ascertain that the decision maker is there. If that person is not there, then we might be wasting our time. The old Soviet communists used the "salami technique" where provisional agreements were constantly referred upstairs for the next superior to demand further concessions.

FINAL WORDS

Pong controlled by aim,
Opponent, context, fears, greed.
Ping has Integrity

Commentary: in the end, it all boils down to integrity. Personal integrity. Companies cannot have integrity, only the people working in them can. Most people's dealings are dictated by fear, emotions, sloth, ego, cowardice, the demands of the situation, the relationship, the opponent, the objective, paying off the mortgage, beckoning pension, the filthy lucre. The person with integrity recognises this, recognises that the values of negotiation are so often murky, so often diametrically opposed to the values of society, but chooses what he uses, how much of it he uses, when he starts and when he stops. The effective negotiator is neither controlled nor driven.

Negotiators?
Pong talkative, weak, poor man.
Ping rich, clever lady.

Commentary: this is the only haiku that reveals that Ping was a woman. One of the few female merchants in Japan at that time. Women often make stronger negotiators than men simply through their ability to listen rather having the macho drive to talk first.

www.ingramcontent.com/pod-product-compliance
Lightning Source LLC
Chambersburg PA
CBHW030813180526
45163CB00003B/1259